PORTRAITS OF GARDEN BEDFELLOWS

A Gardener's Guide
to Plants that Go—
And Grow—Well Together

Elise Laurenzi and Gerald B. Levinson

Photography: Gary Mottau and Elise Laurenzi

Book Design/Development: Ken Silvia and Carol Lasky

PORTRAITS OF GARDEN BEDFELLOWS is published by Corydalis Press, 4 Park Lane, Marblehead, Massachusetts 01945.

For Anne & Agatha

"When the eye is trained to perceive pictorial effect, it is frequently struck by something—some combination of grouping, lighting and colour—that is seen to have that complete aspect of unity and beauty that to the artist's eye forms a picture. Such are the impressions that the artist-gardener endeavors to produce in every portion of the garden."

GERTRUDE JEKYLL, *Colour Schemes for the Flower Garden*

Gardeners and landscaper designers who share Gertrude Jekyll's quest for beautiful "garden pictures" are always searching for the quintessential plant combination. It means experimenting, sometimes failing, but always closely observing and making notes. In some instances the very best effects are made by the simplest means. Often, the most memorable plant grouping is achieved by including a single *special* plant that energizes the entire composition.

The concept for this book began with Jerry's personal desire to create in his own garden "a series of soul-satisfying pictures" and to illustrate some of these in full color. We would like to share with you some twenty favorite plant portraits that can be duplicated by gardeners at any level, using annuals and perennials that are commonly available. With few exceptions, the flowers in this book were grown and photographed in my own garden, as proof that no extra labor or expense is required to combine plants that bring out the best in each other.

We hope you find *Portraits* useful—often.

Elise Laurenzi

Copyright © 1987 by Corydalis Press
Photography © 1987 by Gary Mottau and Elise Laurenzi

Corydalis Press
4 Park Lane
Marblehead, Massachusetts 01945

ISBN 0-9617942-0-8

Library of Congress Catalogue Card Number 86-92069

Printed in the U.S.A.

All rights reserved. No part of this book may be reproduced or transmitted in any form or by any means, electronic or mechanical, including photocopying, recording or by any information storage and retrieval system without premission in writing from the Publisher.

The Quality of Light

"Then there are some days during the summer when the quality of light seems to tend to an extraordinary beauty of effect."

GERTRUDE JEKYLL

Grasses are enjoying a well-deserved horticultural renaissance. They are coming out of the weed patch and into the garden. Many grasses are unsurpassed as specimen or accent plants; their transition from flower to seed is one of the highlights of our gardens.

Over a few weeks in July the gossamer flowers of *Deschampsia* 'Goldgehaenge' evolve from creamy white lace to a golden filigree. In combination with red lilies, nicotiana and spike grass, it fashions a variety of foliage forms, textures and rich brocade colors that persist all summer.

As summer moves into autumn, grasses can be dramatic—even electrifying—when caught in fiery sunsets and lengthening shadows. Then it's time to bring bouquets of dried grasses indoors for an extended season of enjoyment.

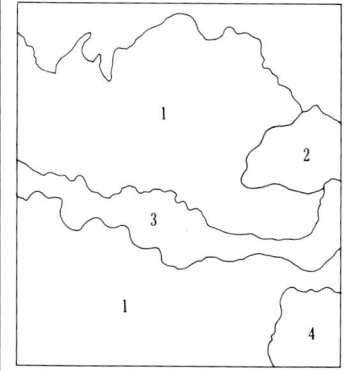

KEY	COMMON NAME	BOTANICAL NAME	HEIGHT	EXPOSURE	SOIL CONDITIONS	APPROXIMATE SPACING	BLOOM TIME	HARDY TO ZONE
1	Tufted Hair Grass	*Deschampsia caespitosa* 'Goldgehaenge'	36"	Sun/light shade	Average to moist soil	24"	June/July	4
2	Spike Grass	*Chasmanthium latifolium*	36"	Sun/light shade	Average to moist soil	24"	August	5
3	Lily	*Lilium* 'Bingo'	36"	Sun/light shade	Average to moist soil	12-15"	July	3
4	Flowering Tobacco	*Nicotiana* 'Nicki Red'	18"	Sun/light shade	Average to moist soil	12"	Summer	Annual

TEXTURE MORE AND MORE

White alyssum is a favorite edger and filler in the summer border. Dressed in colors of pink and purple, its versatility seems endless. This blend of low-growing annuals and perennials resembles a floral carpet of soft colors and refined texture framed by a dark border of purple alyssum. A variety of small flower shapes combine to produce rich patterns within a narrow range of color. Subtle contrasts and highlights are contributed by annual vinca (white) and dusty miller (silver filigree foliage).

Annuals such as alyssum, petunia and lobelia should be sheared and fertilized throughout the summer for more compact form and abundant bloom.

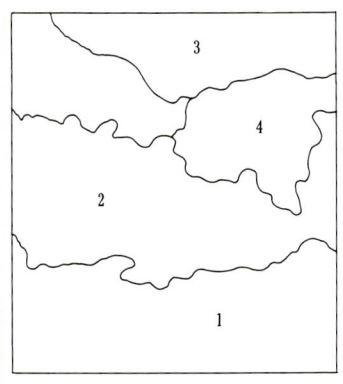

KEY	COMMON NAME	BOTANICAL NAME	HEIGHT	EXPOSURE	SOIL CONDITIONS	APPROXIMATE SPACING	BLOOM TIME	HARDY TO ZONE
1	Sweet Alyssum	*Lobularia maritima* 'Oriental Night'	3-8"	Sun	Average—well-drained	6-8"	Summer	Annual
2	Dusty Miller	*Senecio cineraria* 'Diamond'	10-18"	Sun	Average—well-drained	12"	Summer	Annual
3	Annual Vinca	*Vinca rosea*	12-18"	Sun	Average—well-drained	12"	Summer	Annual
4	Ageratum	*Ageratum* 'Blue Danube'	6-8"	Sun	Average—well-drained	8-10"	Summer	Annual

More Is Not Better (Keep It Simple)

"One plant well chosen can improve a composition, where ten—fighting for light and air—more often result in confusion…"

THOMAS D. CHURCH

It is disappointing that salpiglossis is not used more often. True, it is a bit temperamental for a few days after transplanting into the garden, but patience and nurturing are handsomely rewarded.

The lapidary colors of salpiglossis enhance all the other plants in the border, for hidden in each velvet trumpet are calico marblings of yellow, blue, purple, rose and so forth. In this charming combination, the sobriety of salpiglossis is balanced by the daisy exuberance of feverfew. While not a reliably hardy perennial in colder climates, feverfew furnishes a bounty of self-sown seedlings every spring. Both plants will bloom all summer if pruned or cut and provide a wealth of small bouquets.

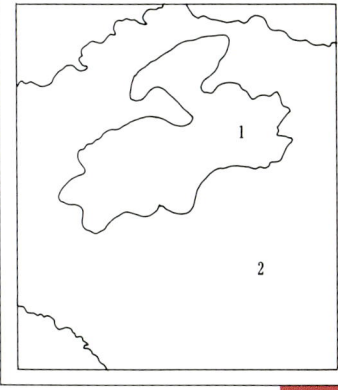

KEY	COMMON NAME	BOTANICAL NAME	HEIGHT	EXPOSURE	SOIL CONDITIONS	APPROXIMATE SPACING	BLOOM TIME	HARDY TO ZONE
1	Painted Tongue	*Salpiglossis sinuata*	24-36"	Sun	Cool summers Average soil	12-15"	Summer	Annual
2	Feverfew	*Chrysanthemum parthenium*	24-36"	Sun	Average soil	15-18"	Summer	4

TEXTURE MORE AND MORE

"As time goes on and gardeners come to see better, they will consider texture more and more. The best results cannot be achieved without it."
FLETCHER STEELE

A color blend of purple red, lavender pink and yellow green? Certainly. The foliage and flower *textures* of bee balm, meadow rue, astilbe and hostas are, as you can see, unrivaled in the shade garden.

As a black line drawing, it would be easier to visualize the patterns these plants contribute to the landscape: tall, airy sprays of meadow rue, dense spikes of astilbe and darker globes of bee balm. Add lacy thalictrum foliage and broad-leaved hostas. Several clumps of hosta at the base give balance and stability to the rather light-headed composition.

If you haven't grown *Astilbe tacquetii* 'Superba', we urge you to do so. This tall, robust plant, with dark green foliage and candelabra of striking pink bloom, is a great performer in the August border.

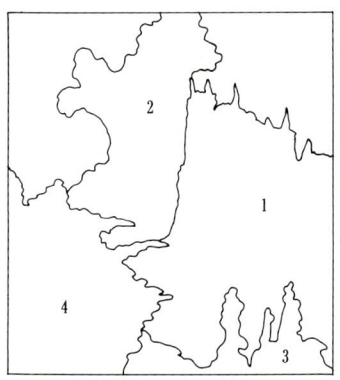

KEY	COMMON NAME	BOTANICAL NAME	HEIGHT	EXPOSURE	SOIL CONDITIONS	APPROXIMATE SPACING	BLOOM TIME	HARDY TO ZONE
1	Garden Spiraea	*Astilbe tacquetii* 'Superba'	36-48"	Light shade	Rich—moist	18"	August	4
2	Meadow Rue	*Thalictrum rochebrunianum*	60-72"	Light shade	Rich—moist	18"	Aug/Sept	4
3	Plantain Lily	*Hosta* 'August Moon'	12-18"	Light shade	Rich—moist	18"	Aug/Sept	3
4	Bee Balm	*Monarda didyma*	30-36"	Light shade	Rich—moist	15"	Jul/Aug	4

TEXTURE MORE AND MORE

Repetition of certain elements in a design unifies the composition. Colors, textures and flower forms in this May grouping are reiterated in many ways using delicate white flower sprays, lacy foliage, graceful plants with arching forms, others with stiff vertical habit. Even the white flower of *Dicentra spectabilis* is a miniature, upside-down version of the lily-flowered tulip.

Apart from these design considerations, this combination is cherished because it blooms over a long period in May, unscathed by spring rains.

Be sure to cut back the withering foliage of tulips and bleeding heart in July and interplant with annuals or late blooming perennials.

KEY	COMMON NAME	BOTANICAL NAME	HEIGHT	EXPOSURE	SOIL CONDITIONS	APPROXIMATE SPACING	BLOOM TIME	HARDY TO ZONE
1	Tulip	*Tulipa* 'Maytime'	24-30"	Sun/light shade	Average—rich soil	6"	May	4
2	Japanese Bleeding Heart	*Dicentra spectabilis* 'Alba'	30-36"	Sun/light shade	Rich—moist soil	24-36"	May/June	3
3	Foamflower	*Tiarella cordifolia*	6-12"	Partial/full shade	Rich—moist soil	10-12"	May/June	3

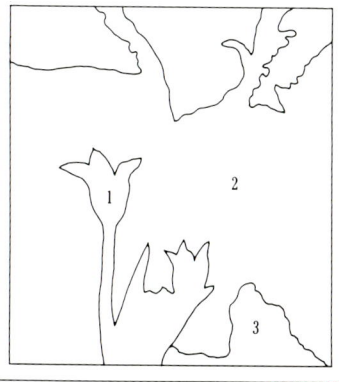

The Pleasures and Hazards of Shade

"Overall the aim should be to maintain some interest in all parts at all seasons, remembering that a plant need not always be in flower to be interesting."
GEORGE E. BROWN

Ferns are indispensable allies in the shade garden, valued more often for form and texture than outstanding color. The Japanese painted fern is choice because it has all these qualities. This fern has been performing to rave reviews ever since it appeared on the American (garden) scene and easily deserves its reputation.

Japanese painted fern has proven hardy and reliable. It transplants easily, adapts to more sun than some other ferns and flourishes in rich, moist soil. Its unusual red and silver markings add highlights to a sombre woodland planting and emphasize the lacy outlines of its foliage. Heightening this effect, we underplanted with blue and white lobelias—carpet annuals that accept the same cultural conditions.

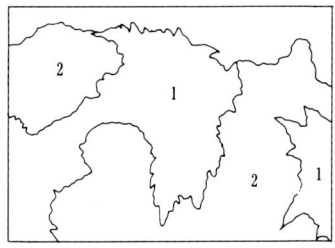

KEY	COMMON NAME	BOTANICAL NAME	HEIGHT	EXPOSURE	SOIL CONDITIONS	APPROXIMATE SPACING	BLOOM TIME	HARDY TO ZONE
1	Japanese Painted Fern	*Athyrium goeringianum* 'Pictum'	15"	Light shade	Rich—moist	15"	Foliage plant	4
2	Lobelia	*Lobelia erinus*	4-6"	Light shade	Average—moist	6-8"	Summer	Annual

Texture More and More

"Search out unusual plants that give individuality and piquance to the garden composition."

JOHN BRIMER

Fennel is not an unusual plant in the kitchen garden, but we rarely see it used in combination with other perennials in the flower border. The fresh green color of its lacy flowers, their unique starburst shape, the feathery foliage and substantial height—these are useful ornamental qualities that should not be overlooked.

Fennel loves to lean on its neighbors, so interplant it with sturdier companions like lilies, dahlias or cannas. On this occasion, its chosen bedfellow is *Althaea* 'Zebrina', a non-stop bloomer with striped mallow flowers.

Other large, decorative herbs you might try are sweet cicely (perennial), dill (annual), angelica (biennial) or comfrey (perennial).

KEY	COMMON NAME	BOTANICAL NAME	HEIGHT	EXPOSURE	SOIL CONDITIONS	APPROXIMATE SPACING	BLOOM TIME	HARDY TO ZONE
1	Striped Mallow	*Althaea* 'Zebrina'	36"	Sun	Average soil	15-18"	Summer	4
2	Fennel	*Foeniculum vulgare*	48-60"	Sun	Average soil	15-18"	Jul/Aug	Annual herb

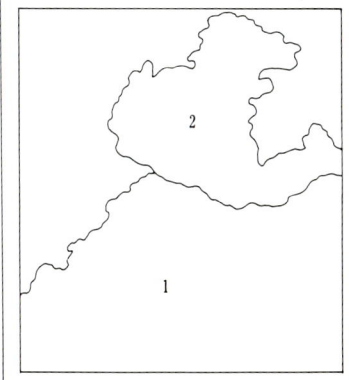

Color Vibes (My Peach is Your Orange)

Flower color is difficult to describe accurately. It changes continuously with the quality and direction of light; the seasons; the texture and age of a blossom as it moves from bud to maturity; the colors of surrounding shrubs and flowers; and, surely, by the limitations of our own language and experience. However you choose to color *Filipendula rubra* 'Venusta' and *Lilium* 'Thunderbolt', be assured that they make a pleasing association for the back of the border and will be the recipient of many compliments.

The lily is delightfully fragrant, especially in the evening, so plant it close to the house or path for greatest enjoyment. Filipendulas are coarse and vigorous growers and will need division long before the lilies.

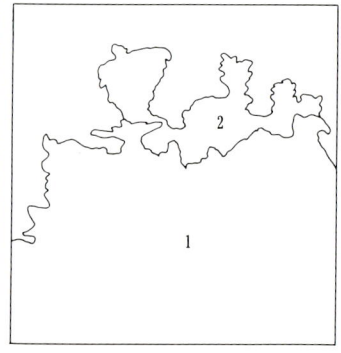

KEY	COMMON NAME	BOTANICAL NAME	HEIGHT	EXPOSURE	SOIL CONDITIONS	APPROXIMATE SPACING	BLOOM TIME	HARDY TO ZONE
1	Lily	*Lilium* 'Thunderbolt'	48-60"	Sun/light shade	Rich, well-drained soil	15-18"	July	3
2	Queen of the Prairie	*Filipendula rubra* 'Venusta'	60-72"	Sun/light shade	Moist soil	24-36"	July	2

THE CANDY STORE

"In May [when] the earth children laugh in multitudes…"
WILLIAM ROBINSON

The month of May is such a storehouse of earthly delights, it is difficult to choose a favorite combination. Jacob's ladder (blue) and wild geranium (pink) are blooming in the company of bleeding heart, foamflower, columbine, squill, globeflower, ferns, wild phlox, trillium, forget-me-not, Virginia bluebells, azaleas… need we go on? Just start with any two of the above and add as many as good design will allow. With time, beautiful colonies will develop into a most pleasing natural landscape.

KEY	COMMON NAME	BOTANICAL NAME	HEIGHT	EXPOSURE	SOIL CONDITIONS	APPROXIMATE SPACING	BLOOM TIME	HARDY TO ZONE
1	Wild Geranium	*Geranium maculatum*	15-18"	Shade	Rich, moist	12-15"	May/June	4
2	Jacob's Ladder	*Polemonium reptans*	12-18"	Shade	Rich, moist	12-15"	May/June	3
3	Globeflower	*Trollius europaeus*	18-24"	Light shade	Moist	10-12"	May/June	3
4	Wild Blue Phlox	*Phlox divaricata*	12-15"	Light shade	Moist	10-12"	May/June	3

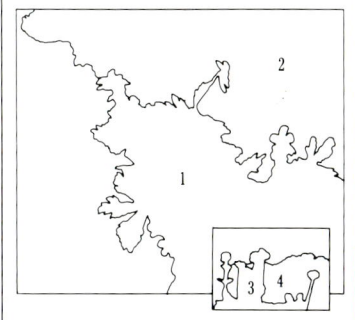

A Change of P(L)ACE

"To some a plant in a free state is more charming than any garden denizen. It is taking care of itself."

WILLIAM ROBINSON

Foxglove and yarrow have leapt the garden wall! In large drifts at the edge of a meadow their contrasting flower shapes and stepped heights create strong horizontal and vertical lines. The effect is softened by a pastel mood—pink candles floating above bands of soft yellow and silver grey.

Here, two perennial favorites are combined in an unfamiliar setting, where they are allowed to grow and spread freely to create their own patterns in the landscape.

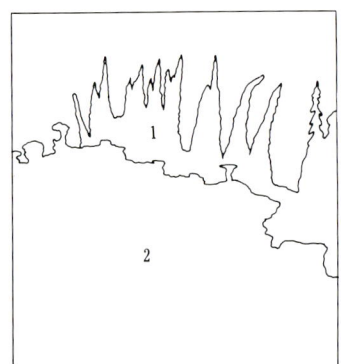

KEY	COMMON NAME	BOTANICAL NAME	HEIGHT	EXPOSURE	SOIL CONDITIONS	APPROXIMATE SPACING	BLOOM TIME	HARDY TO ZONE
1	Foxglove	*Digitalis purpurea*	36-48"	Sun—partial shade	Average—moist	15-18"	June	4 Biennial
2	Yarrow	*Achillea × taygetea* 'Moonshine'	18-24"	Sun—partial shade	Average—well-drained	12-15"	Summer	3

Color Vibes

"All colors are beautiful or ugly according to their quantity in relation to other colors."

FLETCHER STEELE

As an antidote to the overused red salvia/orange marigold combination, we offer this high intensity pairing of yellow *Achillea* 'Moonshine' and orange-red *Cosmos* 'Diablo'. The rich effect of this bed is achieved with a few additions. Notice coreopsis, canna, calendula and celosia, their hot colors moderated somewhat by the foliage of dusty miller and dill.

It was great fun to plan a border with so many colorful annuals. The garden was sizzling all summer long. It also required *daily* dead-heading to keep it picture perfect. Annuals, especially, exact a price for their bountiful, enduring color.

KEY	COMMON NAME	BOTANICAL NAME	HEIGHT	EXPOSURE	SOIL CONDITIONS	APPROXIMATE SPACING	BLOOM TIME	HARDY TO ZONE
1	Yarrow	*Achillea × taygetea* 'Moonshine'	18-24"	Sun/partial shade	Average—well-drained	12-15"	Summer	3
2	Cosmos	*Cosmos sulphureus* 'Diablo'	24-36"	Sun	Average	12-15"	Summer	Annual
3	Plumed Celosia	*Celosia plumosa* 'Gay Feather'	18-24"	Sun	Average—well-drained	12-15"	Summer	Annual
4	Dill	*Anethum graeolens*	24-36"	Sun	Average—well drained	15-18"	Summer	Annual

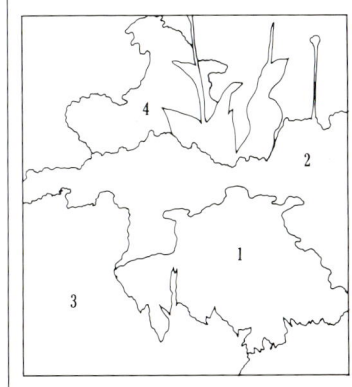

COLOR VIBES

Daylily and bee balm are two delightful plants for any garden. They are well matched for cultural requirements and bloom time, and daylilies are tough enough to ignore the wandering habit of bee balm.

Color combinations can be pale and soft or as fearless as this pair. The colors of *Hemerocallis* 'Hyperion' and *Monarda* 'Cambridge Scarlet' are sharp and clear and strong. In addition, their values are balanced. Such bold punctuation is best used in small quantity for accent. However, in a meadow garden or informal border, framed by a matrix of green foliage, larger drifts are welcome—their fragrance a sweet counterpoint to color.

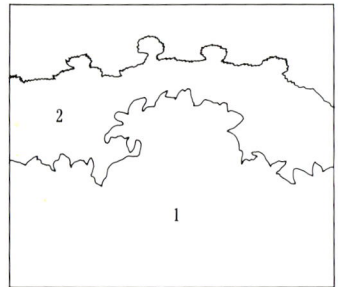

KEY	COMMON NAME	BOTANICAL NAME	HEIGHT	EXPOSURE	SOIL CONDITIONS	APPROXIMATE SPACING	BLOOM TIME	HARDY TO ZONE
1	Daylily	*Hemerocallis* 'Hyperion'	36-40″	Sun/light shade	Average—moist	24-30″	Mid-summer	3
2	Bee Balm	*Monarda didyma* 'Cambridge Scarlet'	36″	Sun/light shade	Average—moist	15-18″	Mid-summer	4

COLOR VIBES

"The eye ... accepts colors only in relation to other colors, whether they be near or remote in the field of vision."
FLETCHER STEELE

Flamboyant azaleas and bulbs are a welcome sight in spring but not always in the same bed. Strident color clashes indicate that the gardener has fallen prey to some catalog hype (perhaps with retouched photographs); the bulbs purchased in October have little to do with the garden in May.

For example, torch azaleas provide some of the most florid accents in the shrub border. Combining them with a cool, white tulip and glaucous blue foliage turns down the thermostat a little.

A few favorite azalea/bulb combinations include: pinkshell azalea with camassia, royal azalea with grape hyacinth, Delaware Valley White azalea with siberian squill and waterlily tulips.

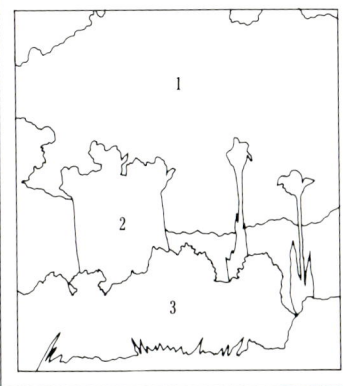

KEY	COMMON NAME	BOTANICAL NAME	HEIGHT	EXPOSURE	SOIL CONDITIONS	APPROXIMATE SPACING	BLOOM TIME	HARDY TO ZONE
1	Torch Azalea	Rhod. kaempferi	72"	Sun/light shade	Rich, moist	60"	May	5
2	Tulip	Tulipa 'Angel'	18"	Sun/light shade	Rich, moist	6"	May	4
3	Wild Phlox	Phlox divaricata 'Alba'	12"	Sun/light shade	Rich, moist	10-12"	May	3

The Pleasures and Hazards of Shade

In shade gardens we leave gaudy colors behind and focus instead on shades of green, foliage patterns, variegation, reflectivity and texture. Success depends on how well we weave these design elements and still pay attention to individual cultural requirements.

Unusual striped foliage and rich, dark red colors make this a striking combination of contrasting effects. The special swirling movement of variegated sedge, like a large pinwheel, lends drama to a mixed shrub border as it uplifts everything around it.

Hosta plantaginea is easy to grow and rarely needs dividing. *Astilbe*, however, may need some "TLC" in the form of extra moisture, fertilization and division every 3 to 4 years to remain vigorous. Still, they are worth the effort. Their *foliage* texture and color are outstanding all season, and they offer a wide range of colors, heights and bloom sequence.

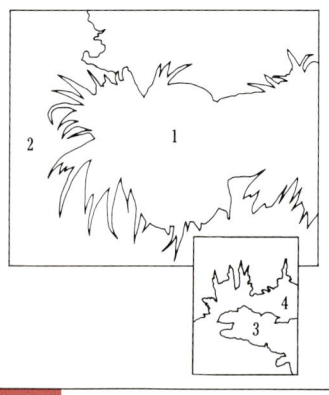

KEY	COMMON NAME	BOTANICAL NAME	HEIGHT	EXPOSURE	SOIL CONDITIONS	APPROXIMATE SPACING	BLOOM TIME	HARDY TO ZONE
1	Japanese Sedge	*Carex Morrowii* 'Aurea-Variegata'	12"	Sun/light shade	Rich, moist	12-15"	Foliage plant	5
2	Impatiens	*Impatiens* 'Fantasia'	8-10"	Light shade	Rich, moist	10-15"	Summer	Annual
3	Plantain Lily	*Hosta plantaginea* 'Grandiflora'	24"	Shade	Rich, moist	18-24"	August	3
4	Garden Spiraea	*Astilbe* 'Montgomery'	36"	Shade	Rich, moist	15-18"	July	4

More Is Not Better (Keep It Simple)

Hosta, one of the best plants for shade, has finally been given a place in the sun. Many of the newer yellow-leaved varieties will grow in half or three-quarter sunlight, making hostas more useful than ever.

Hosta 'August Moon' has foliage of great substance and texture; beautiful shadings from yellow to green create shifting images. Likewise, *Petunia* 'Azure Pearls' is crowded all summer with small trumpets in many tints of the softest blues. It's fascinating to watch these two chameleons in the garden.

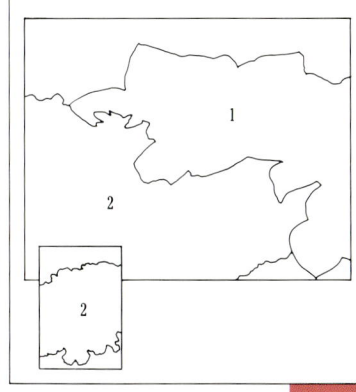

KEY	COMMON NAME	BOTANICAL NAME	HEIGHT	EXPOSURE	SOIL CONDITIONS	APPROXIMATE SPACING	BLOOM TIME	HARDY TO ZONE
1	Plantain Lily	*Hosta* 'August Moon'	18"	Light shade	Moist	18"	Aug/Sept	3
2	Petunia	*Petunia* 'Azure Pearls'	12"	Sun/light shade	Average	10-12"	Summer	Annual

The Candy Store

Tiarella is a diminutive native that can only be described in superlatives. There is no setting in woodland shade that is not the better for this charming ground cover. It is especially memorable with ferns, bleeding heart, columbine or bulbs. Its shallow roots prefer a rich woodland soil with plenty of leafmold; if there are a few rocks or rotting logs to clamber over, so much the better.

What is more, tiarella's versatility does not end at wood's edge. It would be a boon to many urban gardens seeking a sign of grace.

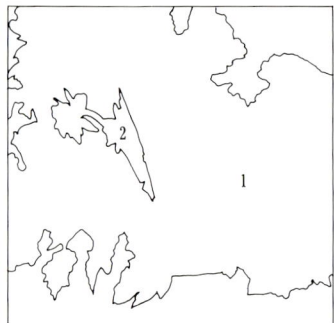

KEY	COMMON NAME	BOTANICAL NAME	HEIGHT	EXPOSURE	SOIL CONDITIONS	APPROXIMATE SPACING	BLOOM TIME	HARDY TO ZONE
1	Foamflower	*Tiarella cordifolia*	10"	Shade	Rich, moist	10"	May/June	4
2	Daffodil	*Narcissus* 'White Lion'	15"	Sun/light shade	Rich, moist	6"	May	4

A Change of P(L)ace

Lavender, pinks and roses were once the mainstay of grand perennial borders. Large manor houses featured roses for garlands and arbors, as natural fountains, pillars and hedges.

For a similar monochromatic theme in a less formal setting you might substitute *Allium schoenprasum, Salvia haematodes* and a hardy shrub rose like 'Therese Bugnet'. All three plants are somewhat coarse and sprawling, but they bloom at the same time in delicious ice cream colors—somewhere between raspberry float and grape smash. With hard pruning for neater, compact plants, the sage and chives will bloom again in July, the rose until frost.

KEY	COMMON NAME	BOTANICAL NAME	HEIGHT	EXPOSURE	SOIL CONDITIONS	APPROXIMATE SPACING	BLOOM TIME	HARDY TO ZONE
1	Chives	*Allium schoenprasum*	18"	Sun	Average	10-12"	June/July	3
2	Meadow Sage	*Salvia haematodes*	36"	Sun	Average	15-18"	June/July	3
3	Rose	*Rosa* 'Therese Bugnet'	60"+	Sun	Rich	60"	June/July+	4

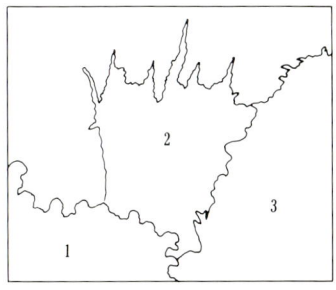

The Quality of Light

As the quality of light changes throughout the day, so does the mood or "theatre" of the garden. An amber wash of late afternoon sun will work its magic on every plant it touches and suffuse foliage and flowers with a rosy aura that is not evident at high noon. At twilight, their color gives way to amethyst shadows. Gardeners soon realize that natural light, capricious and unpredictable, is the true wizard in the landscape.

Two large, vigorous plants like cosmos and reed grass are excellent choices for a meadow or wild garden. They also look rather elegant in a border as filtering sunlight captures and intensifies their warm colors and fine textures.

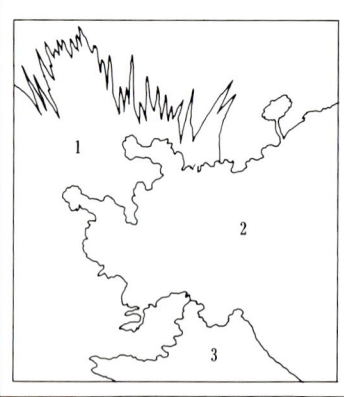

KEY	COMMON NAME	BOTANICAL NAME	HEIGHT	EXPOSURE	SOIL CONDITIONS	APPROXIMATE SPACING	BLOOM TIME	HARDY TO ZONE
1	Feather Reed Grass	*Calamagrostis × acutiflora* 'Stricta'	72"	Sun/light shade	Average—moist	30-36"	June/July	5
2	Cosmos	*Cosmos bipinnatus* 'Sensation'	60"	Sun	Average—moist	15"	Summer	Annual
3	Flowering Tobacco	*Nicotiana* 'Nicki Rose'	18"	Sun/light shade	Average—moist	12"	Summer	Annual